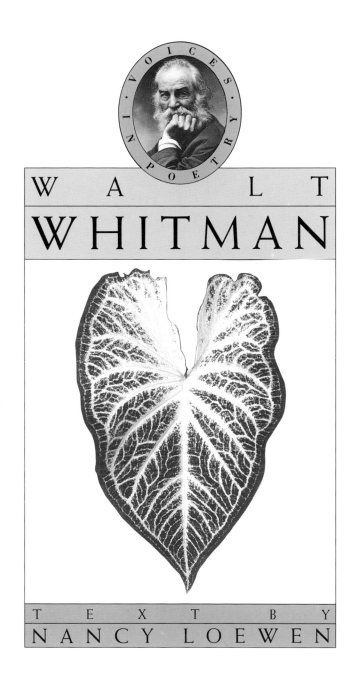

VOICES · IN · POETRY

WALT
WHITMAN

TEXT BY
NANCY LOEWEN

ILLUSTRATIONS BY
ROB DAY

CREATIVE EDITIONS

WHEN I READ THE BOOK

*W*hen I read the book, the biography famous,

And is this then (said I) what the author calls a man's

    life?

And so will some one when I am dead and gone write

    my life?

(As if any man really knew aught of my life,

Why even I myself I often think know little or nothing

    of my real life,

Only a few hints, a few diffused faint clews and

    indirections

I seek for my own use to trace out here.)

From "Inscriptions"
Leaves of Grass

"*It is I you hold and who holds you. I spring from the pages into your arms,*" wrote Walt Whitman in *Leaves of Grass,* a collection of poetry that is regarded as one of the world's literary masterpieces.

In his poems and in his life, Whitman celebrated the human spirit and the human body; he sang the praises of democracy and chronicled the marvel of technological progress. His direct, speechlike writing style and his frank celebration of sensuality shocked many of his contemporaries. But Whitman persisted despite the criticism his unorthodox work received. He spent more than three decades writing, revising, and expanding *Leaves of Grass,* and his influence on the development of modern American poetry has been both profound and enduring.

Walt Whitman.

SONG OF MYSELF

Section 1

I celebrate myself, and sing myself,

And what I assume you shall assume,

For every atom belonging to me as good belongs to you.

I loafe and invite my soul,

I lean and loafe at my ease observing a spear of

summer grass.

My tongue, every atom of my blood, form'd from this

soil, this air,

Born here of parents born here from parents the same,

and their parents the same,

I, now thirty-seven years old in perfect health begin,

Hoping to cease not till death.

Creeds and schools in abeyance,

Retiring back a while sufficed at what they are, but

never forgotten,

I harbor for good or bad, I permit to speak at every

hazard,

Nature without check with original energy.

From "Inscriptions"
Leaves of Grass

CHILDHOOD

Walt Whitman was born on May 31, 1819, in the rural village of West Hills, Long Island, New York. He was the second child of Walter and Louisa Whitman. Of the nine children born to them, one son died in infancy; one was severely retarded; one was insane; one died at a young age of alcoholism and tuberculosis; and, of course, one grew up to join the ranks of the world's greatest poets.

Whitman's earliest memories were infused with the salt smell of the sea and the rhythmic pounding of the Atlantic surf. Alone or with friends, he dug for clams, speared eels, explored inlets, rode the ferries, and tagged along with boat pilots and dockhands. When he was four the family moved to the rapidly expanding city of Brooklyn, where his father worked as a carpenter. The Whitmans returned to Long Island often, however, and both settings were explored in the poet's work.

Walt Whitman's birthplace, Long Island, New York.

*T*here was a child went forth every day,

And the first object he look'd upon, that object he

became,

And that object became part of him for the day or a

certain part of the day,

Or for many years or stretching cycles of years.

The early lilacs became part of this child,

And grass and white and red morning-glories, and

white and red clover, and the song of the

phœbe-bird,

And the Third-month lambs and the sow's pink-faint

litter, and the mare's foal and the cow's calf,

And the noisy brood of the barnyard or by the mire

of the pond-side,

And the fish suspending themselves so curiously below

there, and the beautiful curious liquid,

And the water-plants with their graceful flat heads,

all became part of him.

The field-sprouts of Fourth-month and Fifth-month

became part of him,

Winter-grain sprouts and those of the light-yellow

corn, and the esculent roots of the garden,

(continued)

And the apple-trees cover'd with blossoms and the
      fruit afterward, and wood-berries, and the
      commonest weeds by the road,
And the old drunkard staggering home from the out-
      house of the tavern whence he had lately risen,
And the schoolmistress that pass'd on her way to the
      school,
And the friendly boys that pass'd, and the quarrelsome
      boys,
And the tidy and fresh-cheek'd girls, and the barefoot
      negro boy and girl,
And all the changes of city and country wherever he went.

His own parents, he that had father'd him and she that
      had conceiv'd him in her womb and birth'd him,
They gave this child more of themselves than that,
They gave him afterward every day, they became part
      of him.

The mother at home quietly placing the dishes on the
      supper-table,
The mother with mild words, clean her cap and gown, a
      wholesome odor falling off her person and
      clothes as she walks by,
The father, strong, self-sufficient, manly, mean, anger'd,
      unjust,
The blow, the quick loud word, the tight bargain, the
      crafty lure,
The family usages, the language, the company, the
      furniture, the yearning and swelling heart,

Affection that will not be gainsay'd, the sense of what is
real, the thought if after all it should prove unreal,

The doubts of day-time and the doubts of night-time,
the curious whether and how,

Whether that which appears so is so, or is it all flashes
and specks?

Men and women crowding fast in the streets, if they
are not flashes and specks what are they?

The streets themselves and the façades of houses, and
goods in the windows,

Vehicles, teams, the heavy-plank'd wharves, the huge
crossing at the ferries,

The village on the highland seen from afar at sunset,
the river between,

Shadows, aureola and mist, the light falling on roofs
and gables of white or brown two miles off,

The schooner near by sleepily dropping down the tide,
the little boat slack-tow'd astern,

The hurrying tumbling waves, quick-broken crests,
slapping,

The strata of color'd clouds, the long bar of maroon-
tint away solitary by itself, the spread of purity
it lies motionless in,

The horizon's edge, the flying sea-crow, the fragrance
of salt marsh and shore mud,

These became part of that child who went forth every
day, and who now goes, and will always go
forth every day.

From "Autumn Rivulets"
Leaves of Grass

*W*hitman attended public schools in Brooklyn, where his teachers labeled him "a dreamy and impractical youth." At age eleven he left school and began working as an office boy at a small law firm. One of the lawyers, Whitman remembered gratefully, "help'd me at my handwriting and composition, and, (the signal event of my life up to that time,) subscribed for me to a big circulating library." Whitman became an avid reader and would remain so the rest of his life.

At age twelve he began a printing apprenticeship at a New York newspaper. Like Benjamin Franklin and Mark Twain, Whitman received much of his education standing before a hand press, setting lines of type letter by letter. Sometimes he contributed short items to the paper. These small successes so bolstered his courage that he submitted an anonymous article to the *New York Mirror*. His hands trembled as he opened the pages containing his work. "How it made my heart double-beat to see my *piece* on the pretty white paper, in nice type," he later recalled.

Winter in Brooklyn.

When I heard the learn'd astronomer,

When the proofs, the figures, were ranged in

columns before me,

When I was shown the charts and diagrams, to add,

divide, and measure them,

When I sitting heard the astronomer where he

lectured with much applause in the lecture-

room,

How soon unaccountable I became tired and sick,

Till rising and gliding out I wander'd off by myself,

In the mystical moist night-air, and from time to time,

Look'd up in perfect silence at the stars.

From "By the Roadside"
Leaves of Grass

SCHOOLMASTER

*W*hitman graduated as a journeyman printer at the age of sixteen, but he wasn't able to practice his trade right away. In 1835 fire ravaged New York's publishing district; later that year a second fire destroyed nearly seven hundred buildings and threw the city into an economic tailspin. Unable to find work, Whitman returned to his family, then farming on Long Island. But Whitman refused to do farmwork, much to his father's angry bewilderment. Instead, he became a school-teacher, taking on a series of short appointments in one-room country schoolhouses across Long Island.

The curriculum was basic, and Whitman was casual about his teaching duties, preferring open discussions and games of Twenty Questions to more disciplined approaches. While the terms were in session he "boarded round," living a few days at his students' homes, often sleeping on straw mattresses in drafty corners. He was lonely much of the time, but later came to appreciate this period as "one of my best experiences and deepest lessons in human nature behind the scenes, and in the masses."

New York City on fire, December 10, 1835.

ONE'S-SELF I SING

One's-self I sing, a simple separate person,
Yet utter the word Democratic, the word En-Masse.

Of physiology from top to toe I sing,
Not physiognomy alone nor brain alone is worthy for
    the Muse,
        I say the Form complete is worthier far,
The Female equally with the Male I sing.

Of Life immense in passion, pulse, and power,
Cheerful, for freest action form'd under the laws
    divine,
The Modern Man I sing.

From "Inscriptions"
Leaves of Grass

PUBLISHER

At nineteen, Whitman bought a secondhand press, rented an office above a stable, and started his own weekly newspaper, the *Long Islander*. The paper contained articles reprinted from larger papers, as well as local-interest stories about prize pumpkins, three-legged cows, and the like. Whitman delivered the papers himself, riding his white mare, Nina, and visiting with the farm families as he went along. "I never had happier jaunts," he noted.

After a year, however, Whitman became restless and sold the paper. For many years he bounced from job to job, working for various newspapers as a printer and often as an editor. He did good work, but had a reputation for sloth. "There is a man about our office so lazy that it takes two men to open his jaws when he speaks," gibed the management of the *Aurora*, a New York daily. "If you kick him he's too idle to cry, for then he'd have to wipe his eyes. *What* can be done with him?"

Men at work in a print shop.

*T*his is what you shall do: Love the earth and sun and the animals, despise riches, give alms to every one that asks, stand up for the stupid and crazy, devote your income and labor to others, hate tyrants, argue not concerning God, have patience and indulgence toward the people, take off your hat to nothing known or unknown or to any man or number of men, go freely with powerful uneducated persons and with the young and with the mothers of families, read these leaves in the open air every season of every year of your life, re-examine all you have been told at school or church or in any book, dismiss whatever insults your own soul, and your very flesh shall be a great poem and have the richest fluency not only in its words but in the silent lines of its lips and face and between the lashes of your eyes and in every motion and joint of your body.

From the preface
to the 1855 edition of
Leaves of Grass

*W*hitman may have been lackadaisical about his work sometimes, but he still managed to accomplish a great deal. Between newspaper jobs he published short stories, poems, and essays in popular magazines; he even published a temperance novel, *Franklin Evans*, as an extra edition of a local paper. Above all he enjoyed the city of New York. Dressed like a dandy with a top hat, cane, and a flower in his lapel, Whitman adopted the air of a gentleman and immersed himself in the city's parks, theaters, music, art, and opera.

Whitman was also an active member of the Democratic Party and once addressed a rally of fifteen thousand people. Slavery was the burning question of the day and, for a time, split the party into disputing factions. Whitman joined the Free Soil Democrats, who believed that slavery should be prohibited from all annexed territories. But his outspoken beliefs cost him several important editorial positions, and as he entered his thirties he became disillusioned with political parties and with journalism.

A torchlight procession marches past New York City's Tammany Hall.

It is the fashion among dillettants and fops (perhaps I myself am not guiltless,) to decry the whole formulation of the active politics of America, as beyond redemption, and to be carefully kept away from. See you that you do not fall into this error. America, it may be, is doing very well upon the whole, notwithstanding these antics of the parties and their leaders, these half-brain'd nominees, the many ignorant ballots, and many elected failures and blatherers. It is the dillettants, and all who shirk their duty, who are not doing well. As for you, I advise you to enter more strongly yet into politics. I advise every young man to do so. Always inform yourself; always do the best you can; always vote. Disengage yourself from parties. They have been useful, and to some extent remain so; but the floating, uncommitted electors, farmers, clerks, mechanics, the masters of parties—watching aloof, inclining victory this side or that side—such are the ones most needed, present and future. For America, if eligible at all to downfall and ruin, is eligible within herself, not without; for I see clearly that the combined foreign world could not beat her down. But these savage, wolfish parties alarm me. Owning no law but their own will, more and more combative, less and less tolerant of the idea of ensemble and of equal brotherhood, the perfect equality of the States, the ever-over-arching American ideas, it behooves you to convey yourself implicitly to no party, nor submit blindly to their dictators, but steadily hold yourself judge and master over all of them.

From *Democratic Vistas*

E M E R G E N C E

Trading in his top coat and cane for laborer's denim and a wide-brimmed hat, Whitman did a little carpentry work with his father and brothers, speculated in real estate, and for a while operated his own print shop. Other young men were heading west, seeking adventure and California gold, but Whitman was content among the myriad faces on the streets of his city. He rode stagecoaches just to talk to the drivers; his friends included mechanics and ferryboat hands. In all his doings he carried with him a notebook in order to more easily capture his thoughts. Gradually the jottings became more urgent. Wrote biographer Justin Kaplan, "In his green notebook the printer, schoolmaster, fiction writer, editor, shopkeeper, and housebuilder began—for the first time, as far as anyone knows—to sound his voice over the roofs of the world."

A daguerreotype of Walt Whitman, c. 1850.

This is the meal equally set, this the meat for
natural hunger,
It is for the wicked just the same as the righteous, I
make appointments with all,
I will not have a single person slighted or left away,
The kept-woman, sponger, thief, are hereby invited,
The heavy-lipp'd slave is invited, the venerealee is
invited;
There shall be no difference between them and the rest.

This is the press of a bashful hand, this the float and
odor of hair,
This the touch of my lips to yours, this the murmur of
yearning,

This the far-off depth and height reflecting my own face,
This the thoughtful merge of myself, and the outlet again.

Do you guess I have some intricate purpose?
Well I have, for the Fourth-month showers have, and
the mica on the side of a rock has.

Do you take it I would astonish?
Does the daylight astonish? does the early redstart
twittering through the woods?
Do I astonish more than they?

This hour I tell things in confidence,
I might not tell everybody, but I will tell you.

From "Inscriptions"
Leaves of Grass

LEAVES OF GRASS

*B*y 1855, Walt Whitman was finally ready to reveal the ecstatic utterings of his notebooks to the American public. Conventional publishers weren't interested in his unusual book, however, so he hired some friends to print it and actually set a number of pages himself. The first edition of *Leaves of Grass* was ninety-five pages long and contained twelve untitled poems. The frontispiece was an engraved photograph of the thirty-six-year-old poet: a man with a short beard and jaunty hat who defied the formal conventions of the period by appearing in his shirtsleeves with his collar open, revealing the edge of his flannel undershirt.

Leaves of Grass was largely ignored, but among those who did read it, reaction was strong on both sides. A Boston paper attributed the book to an escaped lunatic. The poet John Greenleaf Whittier reportedly threw his copy into the fire. "One cannot leave it about for chance readers," said critic Charles Eliot Norton, "and would be sorry to know that any woman had looked into it past the title-page."

Others were moved and inspired by the book. "This man has brave stuff in him," one reviewer observed. Ralph Waldo Emerson, a well-respected poet and essayist, wrote Whitman a letter of highest praise. "I have great joy in it," he stated. "I greet you at the beginning of a great career, which yet must have had a long foreground somewhere, for such a start."

Although Whitman was to write two books of prose, he considered *Leaves of Grass* to be his life's work. He continually revised and expanded the book, publishing nine editions before his death in 1892.

The frontispiece of the first edition of Leaves of Grass.

SONG OF MYSELF

From Section 24

*W*alt Whitman, a kosmos, of Manhattan the son,

Turbulent, fleshy, sensual, eating, drinking and

     breeding,

No sentimentalist, no stander above men and women

     or apart from them,

No more modest than immodest.

Unscrew the locks from the doors!

Unscrew the doors themselves from their jambs!

Whoever degrades another degrades me,

And whatever is done or said returns at last to me.

Through me the afflatus surging and surging,

     through me the current and index.

I speak the pass-word primeval, I give the sign of

     democracy,

By God! I will accept nothing which all cannot have

     their counterpart of on the same terms.

Through me many long dumb voices,

Voices of the interminable generations of prisoners

     and slaves,

Voices of the diseas'd and despairing and of thieves

     and dwarfs,

Voices of cycles of preparation and accretion,

And of the threads that connect the stars, and of wombs

     and of the father-stuff,

And of the rights of them the others are down upon,

Of the deform'd, trivial, flat, foolish, despised,

Fog in the air, beetles rolling balls of dung.

Through me forbidden voices,

Voices of sexes and lusts, voices veil'd and I remove

     the veil,

Voices indecent by me clarified and transfigur'd.

From "Inscriptions"
Leaves of Grass

THE CIVIL WAR

*T*oward midnight on April 12, 1861, Walt Whitman was walking down Broadway after a night at the opera when he heard the sharp cries of newsboys hawking extra editions. The Confederates had opened fire on Fort Sumter in Charleston, South Carolina. It was the start of the Civil War.

At forty-two, the graybearded Whitman was too old to enlist, but his younger brother George did. In December 1862, following intense fighting at Fredericksburg, Virginia, Whitman saw his brother's misspelled name on a list of wounded and rushed to the camp hospitals to find him. George Whitman was only superficially injured and had already recovered by the time Whitman got to him, but Whitman remained in camp for more than a week, helping to care for the wounded. In his journal he wrote:

> *The results of the late battle are exhibited every-where about here in thousands of cases, (hundreds die every day), in the camp, brigade, and division hospitals. These are merely tents, and sometimes very poor ones, the wounded lying on the ground, lucky if their blankets are spread on layers of pine or hemlock twigs, or small leaves. No cots; seldom even a mattress. It is pretty cold. The ground is frozen hard, and there is occasional snow. I go around from one case to another. I do not see that I do much good to these wounded and dying; but I cannot leave them. Once in a while some youngster holds on to me convulsively, and I do what I can for him; at any rate, stop with him and sit near him for hours, if he wishes it.*

The bombardment of Fredericksburg.

While my wife at my side lies slumbering, and
    the wars are over long,
And my head on the pillow rests at home, and the
    vacant midnight passes,
And through the stillness, through the dark, I hear,
    just hear, the breath of my infant,
There in the room as I wake from sleep this vision
    presses upon me;
The engagement opens there and then in fantasy
    unreal,
The skirmishers begin, they crawl cautiously ahead,
    I hear the irregular snap! snap!
I hear the sounds of the different missiles, the short
    t-h-t! t-h-t! of the rifle-balls,
I see the shells exploding leaving small white clouds,
    I hear the great shells shrieking as they pass,
The grape like the hum and whirr of wind through the
    trees, (tumultuous now the contest rages,)

All the scenes at the batteries rise in detail before me
again,

The crashing and smoking, the pride of the men in their
pieces,

The chief-gunner ranges and sights his piece and
selects a fuse of the right time,

After firing I see him lean aside and look eagerly off to
note the effect;

Elsewhere I hear the cry of a regiment charging, (the
young colonel leads himself this time with
brandish'd sword,)

I see the gaps cut by the enemy's volleys, (quickly fill'd
up, no delay,)

I breathe the suffocating smoke, then the flat clouds
hover low concealing all;

Now a strange lull for a few seconds, not a shot fired
on either side,

Then resumed the chaos louder than ever, with eager
calls and orders of officers,

(continued)

While from some distant part of the field the wind wafts to my ears a shout of applause, (some special success,)

And ever the sound of the cannon far or near, (rousing even in dreams a devilish exultation and all the old mad joy in the depths of my soul,)

And ever the hastening of infantry shifting positions, batteries, cavalry, moving hither and thither,

(The falling, dying, I heed not, the wounded dripping and red I heed not, some to the rear are hobbling,)

Grime, heat, rush, aides-de-camp galloping by or on a full run,

With the patter of small arms, the warning *s-s-t* of the rifles, (these in my vision I hear or see,)

And bombs bursting in air, and at night the vari-color'd rockets.

From "Drum-Taps"
Leaves of Grass

The Civil War became for Whitman a personal mission of brotherhood and love. He moved to Washington, D.C., took a part-time job as a secretary in the Army Paymaster's Office, and spent the rest of his time visiting soldiers. He dressed their wounds, read to them, and wrote letters home for those who weren't able to write. As he went about his wartime work, Whitman transformed his emotions and experiences into a collection of poems called "Drum-Taps."

On Good Friday, April 14, 1865, five days after Lee's surrender ended the Civil War, President Abraham Lincoln was shot in Washington; he died the next day. Whitman was visiting his mother in Brooklyn at the time, and it was with sorrow and disbelief that they read about the tragedy in the papers. "Mother prepared breakfast—and other meals afterward—as usual; but not a mouthful was eaten all day by either of us," Whitman wrote. "We each drank half a cup of coffee; that was all. Little was said. We got every newspaper morning and evening, and the frequent extras of that period, and pass'd them silently to each other."

Whitman soon composed one of his best-known poems, "When Lilacs Last in the Dooryard Bloom'd," as a moving tribute to the slain leader.

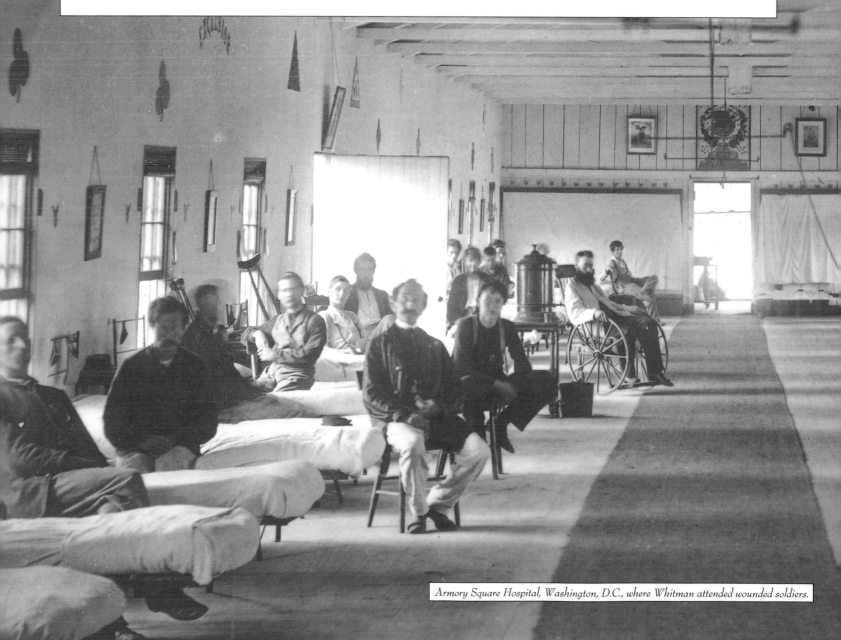

Armory Square Hospital, Washington, D.C., where Whitman attended wounded soldiers.

1

*W*hen lilacs last in the dooryard bloom'd,

And the great star early droop'd in the western sky

   in the night,

I mourn'd, and yet shall mourn with ever-returning

   spring.

Ever-returning spring, trinity sure to me you bring,

Lilac blooming perennial and drooping star in the west,

And thought of him I love.

2

O powerful western fallen star!

O shades of night—O moody, tearful night!

O great star disappear'd—O the black murk that hides

   the star!

O cruel hands that hold me powerless—O helpless

   soul of me!

O harsh surrounding cloud that will not free my soul.

3

In the dooryard fronting an old farm-house near the

   white-wash'd palings,

Stands the lilac-bush tall-growing with heart-shaped

   leaves of rich green,

With many a pointed blossom rising delicate, with the

   perfume strong I love,

With every leaf a miracle—and from this bush in the

   dooryard,

With delicate-color'd blossoms and heart-shaped leaves

   of rich green,

A sprig with its flower I break.

4

In the swamp in secluded recesses,

A shy and hidden bird is warbling a song.

Solitary the thrush,

The hermit withdrawn to himself, avoiding the

   settlements,

Sings by himself a song.

Song of the bleeding throat,

Death's outlet song of life, (for well dear brother I know,

If thou wast not granted to sing thou would'st surely die.)

5

Over the breast of the spring, the land, amid cities,

Amid lanes and through old woods, where lately

     the violets peep'd from the ground, spotting the

     gray debris,

Amid the grass in the fields each side of the lanes,

     passing the endless grass,

Passing the yellow-spear'd wheat, every grain from

     its shroud in the dark-brown fields uprisen,

Passing the apple-tree blows of white and pink in the

     orchards,

Carrying a corpse to where it shall rest in the grave,

Night and day journeys a coffin.

6

Coffin that passes through lanes and streets,

Through day and night with the great cloud darken-

     ing the land,

With the pomp of the inloop'd flags with the cities

     draped in black,

With the show of the States themselves as of crape-

     veil'd women standing,

With processions long and winding and the flambeaus

     of the night,

With the countless torches lit, with the silent sea of faces

     and the unbared heads,

With the waiting depot, the arriving coffin, and the

     sombre faces,

With dirges through the night, with the thousand

     voices rising strong and solemn,

With all the mournful voices of the dirges pour'd

     around the coffin,

The dim-lit churches and the shuddering organs—

     where amid these you journey,

With the tolling tolling bells' perpetual clang,

Here, coffin that slowly passes,

I give you my sprig of lilac.

From "Memories of President Lincoln"
Leaves of Grass

31

Whitman in his later years.

GOOD GRAY POET

For ten years, Whitman made his home in Washington, D.C. He took a job as a clerk in the Department of the Interior, but his position came to an abrupt end when James Harlan was appointed Secretary of the Interior. Dozens of government workers lost their jobs as Secretary Harlan reorganized the department for efficiency. Whitman's dismissal was different, however. Tipped off that Whitman had written a radical book of poetry, Secretary Harlan rifled through Whitman's desk and found a copy of *Leaves of Grass* in a drawer. A quick perusal confirmed his suspicion that the book was indecent. "I will not have the author of that book in this Department," he proclaimed.

By this time Whitman was able to rely on a number of influential allies who took up his cause, and within twenty-four hours he had a new job at the Attorney General's Office. The incident prompted fellow writer and friend William O'Connor to write a forty-six-page pamphlet championing Whitman as the poet of the American people. It was called *The Good Gray Poet*—a title by which Whitman is still known today.

TO A CERTAIN CIVILIAN

*D*id you ask dulcet rhymes from me?

Did you seek the civilian's peaceful and languishing

rhymes?

Did you find what I sang erewhile so hard to follow?

Why I was not singing erewhile for you to follow, to

understand—nor am I now;

(I have been born of the same as the war was born,

The drum-corps' rattle is ever to me sweet music,

I love well the martial dirge,

With slow wail and convulsive throb leading the

officer's funeral;)

What to such as you anyhow such a poet as I?

therefore leave my works,

And go lull yourself with what you can understand,

and with piano-tunes,

For I lull nobody, and you will never understand me.

From "Drum-Taps"
Leaves of Grass

33

*O*n a January night in 1873, Walt Whitman woke up in his fourth-floor Washington apartment to find himself partially paralyzed. A stroke had brought an end to the robust health of which he'd been so proud. That misfortune was soon followed by another: his mother died in May, an event Whitman called "the great dark cloud of my life."

Depressed and unable to work, Whitman moved in with his brother George's family in Camden, New Jersey. The two brothers quarreled often, the clash of the businessman and the poet. "I am very comfortable here indeed, but my *heart* is blank and lonesome utterly," Whitman confided to a friend.

Beginning in 1876 he turned to another family for strength. The Staffords lived on a nearby farm; Whitman was a frequent and welcome guest. "Am with folks I love, & that love me," he noted after a visit. "Have had a real good old-fashion'd time, first-rate for me—It is a farm, every thing plain & plenty, & blazing wood fires." During the summers he spent long hours outdoors, enjoying the meadows and woods. Gradually his health and spirits improved, and he later wrote about his recuperative experience in *Specimen Days*.

"The Lowland Brook" by Howard Pyle, c. 1880.

$\mathcal{S}$unday, Aug. 27. – Another day quite free from mark'd prostration and pain. It seems indeed as if peace and nutriment from heaven subtly filter into me as I slowly hobble down these country lanes and across fields, in the good air—as I sit here in solitude with Nature—open, voiceless, mystic, far removed, yet palpable, eloquent Nature. . . . Shall I tell you, reader, to what I attribute my already much-restored health? That I have been almost two years, off and on, without drugs and medicines, and daily in the open air. Last summer I found a particularly secluded little dell off one side by my creek, originally a large dug-out marl-pit, now abandon'd, fill'd with bushes, trees, grass, a group of willows, a straggling bank, and a spring of delicious water running right through the middle of it, with two or three little cascades. Here I retreated every hot day, and follow it up this summer. Here I realize the meaning of that old fellow who said he was seldom less alone than when alone. Never before did I get so close to Nature; never before did she come so close to me.

From *Specimen Days*

*I*n 1884, at the age of sixty-five, Whitman bought a small house in Camden, New Jersey. It was located near a railroad and a fertilizer factory, but Whitman didn't complain: the house on Mickle Street was his first real home, and it would be the last.

Surrounded by boxes, papers, and books, Whitman reviewed his many journals and edited his life—ripping out pages, crossing out words, changing initials to numbers. Certain things, he explained to a visitor, were "too sacred—too surely and only mine—to be perpetuated." For this reason, much about Whitman's life remains an enigma. He enhanced the mystery by claiming offhandedly to have fathered six children and by alluding to a love affair that ended in an "enforced separation." On the other hand, it is clear that his deepest emotional attachments were to men, and he seems to have gone through periods of anxiety related to sexual ambiguity.

Whitman's friends made sure that he was not left alone in his old age. Some of them pitched in to buy him a buggy and a sorrel pony, and Whitman took great pleasure in his daily outings. In 1888, however, the jaunts came to an abrupt end when Whitman suffered another series of strokes. Too crippled to get around, Whitman hired a widow to care for him in exchange for her rent. His neighbor, a young man named Horace Traubel, ran errands for him and became his confidante, recording many conversations with him. Visitors came often to the little house on Mickle Street—literary intellectuals as well as the cab drivers and laborers whose company Whitman so enjoyed.

Camden, New Jersey: Walt Whitman's home.

*N*ot to exclude or demarcate, or pick out evils

from their formidable masses (even to

expose them,)

But add, fuse, complete, extend—and celebrate the

immortal and the good.

Haughty this song, its words and scope,

To span vast realms of space and time,

Evolution—the cumulative   growths and generations.

Begun in ripen'd youth and steadily pursued,

Wandering, peering, dallying with all—war, peace, day

and night absorbing,

Never even for one brief hour abandoning my task,

I end it here in sickness, poverty, and old age.

I sing of life, yet mind me well of death:

To-day shadowy Death dogs my steps, my seated

shape, and has for years—

Draws sometimes close to me, as face to face.

From "Second Annex: Good-bye My Fancy"
Leaves of Grass

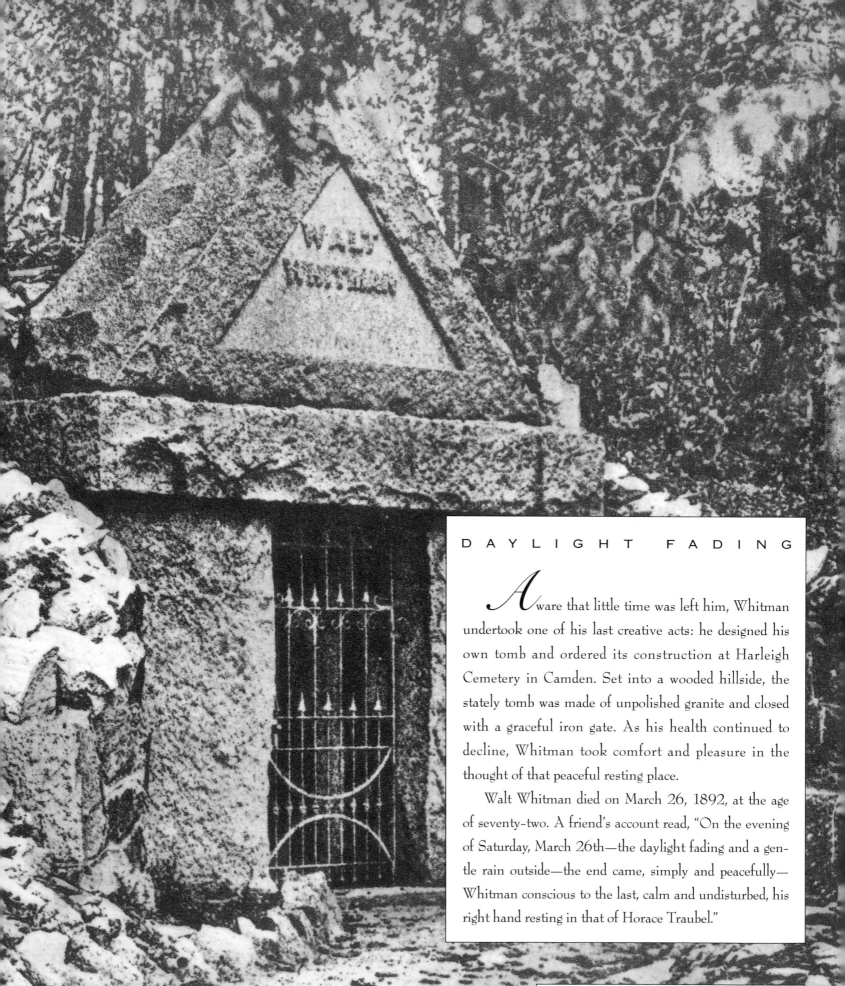

DAYLIGHT FADING

*A*ware that little time was left him, Whitman undertook one of his last creative acts: he designed his own tomb and ordered its construction at Harleigh Cemetery in Camden. Set into a wooded hillside, the stately tomb was made of unpolished granite and closed with a graceful iron gate. As his health continued to decline, Whitman took comfort and pleasure in the thought of that peaceful resting place.

Walt Whitman died on March 26, 1892, at the age of seventy-two. A friend's account read, "On the evening of Saturday, March 26th—the daylight fading and a gentle rain outside—the end came, simply and peacefully—Whitman conscious to the last, calm and undisturbed, his right hand resting in that of Horace Traubel."

Whitman's tomb at Harleigh Cemetery, Camden, New Jersey.

Out of the cradle endlessly rocking,

Out of the mocking-bird's throat, the musical shuttle,

Out of the Ninth-month midnight,

Over the sterile sands and the fields beyond, where
    the child leaving his bed wander'd alone,
    bareheaded, barefoot,

Down from the shower'd halo,

Up from the mystic play of shadows twining and
    twisting as if they were alive,

Out from the patches of briers and blackberries,

From the memories of the bird that chanted to me,

From your memories sad brother, from the fitful risings
    and fallings I heard,

From under that yellow half-moon late-risen and
    swollen as if with tears,

From those beginning notes of yearning and love there
    in the mist,

From the thousand responses of my heart never to
    cease,

From the myriad thence-arous'd words,

From the word stronger and more delicious than any,

From such as now they start the scene revisiting,

As a flock, twittering, rising, or overhead passing,

Borne hither, ere all eludes me, hurriedly,

A man, yet by these tears a little boy again,

Throwing myself on the sand, confronting the waves,

I, chanter of pains and joys, uniter of here and
    hereafter,

Taking all hints to use them, but swiftly leaping
    beyond them,

A reminiscence sing.

Once Paumanok,

When the lilac-scent was in the air and Fifth-month
    grass was growing,

Up this seashore in some briers,

Two feather'd guests from Alabama, two together,

And their nest, and four light-green eggs spotted
    with brown,

And every day the he-bird to and fro near at hand,

And every day the she-bird crouch'd on her nest,
    silent, with bright eyes,

(continued)

And every day I, a curious boy, never too close, never

      disturbing them,

Cautiously peering, absorbing, translating.

Shine! shine! shine!

Pour down your warmth, great sun!

While we bask, we two together.

Two together!

Winds blow south, or winds blow north,

Day come white, or night come black,

Home, or rivers and mountains from home,

Singing all time, minding no time,

While we two keep together.

Till of a sudden,

May-be kill'd, unknown to her mate,

One forenoon the she-bird crouch'd not on the nest,

Nor return'd that afternoon, nor the next,

Nor ever appear'd again.

And thenceforward all summer in the sound of the sea,

And at night under the full of the moon in calmer

      weather,

Over the hoarse surging of the sea,

Or flitting from brier to brier by day,

I saw, I heard at intervals the remaining one, the

      he-bird,

The solitary guest from Alabama.

Blow! blow! blow!

Blow up sea-winds along Paumanok's shore;

I wait and I wait till you blow my mate to me.

Yes, when the stars glisten'd,

All night long on the prong of a moss-scallop'd stake,

Down almost amid the slapping waves,

Sat the lone singer wonderful causing tears.

He call'd on his mate,

He pour'd forth the meanings which I of all men know.

Yes my brother I know,

The rest might not, but I have treasur'd every note,

For more than once dimly down to the beach gliding,

Silent, avoiding the moonbeams, blending myself

       with the shadows,

Recalling now the obscure shapes, the echoes, the

       sounds and sights after their sorts,

The white arms out in the breakers tirelessly tossing,

I, with bare feet, a child, the wind wafting my hair,

Listen'd long and long.

Listen'd to keep, to sing, now translating the notes,

Following you my brother.

Soothe! soothe! soothe!

Close on its wave soothes the wave behind,

And again another behind embracing and lapping,

      every one close,

But my love soothes not me, not me.

Low hangs the moon, it rose late,

It is lagging—O I think it is heavy with love, with love.

O madly the sea pushes upon the land,

With love, with love.

O night! do I not see my love fluttering out

      among the breakers?

What is that little black thing I see there in the white?

Loud! loud! loud!

Loud I call to you, my love!

High and clear I shoot my voice over the waves,

Surely you must know who is here, is here,

You must know who I am, my love.

Low-hanging moon!

What is that dusky spot in your brown yellow?

O it is the shape, the shape of my mate!

(continued)

O moon do not keep her from me any longer.

Land! land! O land!
Whichever way I turn, O I think you could give me my
      mate back again if you only would,
For I am almost sure I see her dimly whichever way
      I look.

O rising stars!
Perhaps the one I want so much will rise, will rise
      with some of you.

O throat! O trembling throat!
Sound clearer through the atmosphere!
Pierce the woods, the earth,
Somewhere listening to catch you must be the one
      I want.

Shake out carols!
Solitary here, the night's carols!

Carols of lonesome love! death's carols!
Carols under that lagging, yellow, waning moon!
O under that moon where she droops almost down into
      the sea!
O reckless despairing carols.

But soft! sink low!
Soft! let me just murmur,
And do you wait a moment you husky-nois'd sea,
For somewhere I believe I heard my mate responding
      to me,
So faint, I must be still, be still to listen,
But not altogether still, for then she might not come
      immediately to me.

Hither my love!
Here I am! here!
With this just-sustain'd note I announce myself to you,
This gentle call is for you my love, for you.

Do not be decoy'd elsewhere,

That is the whistle of the wind, it is not my voice,

That is the fluttering, the fluttering of the spray,

Those are the shadows of leaves.

O darkness! O in vain!

O I am very sick and sorrowful.

O brown halo in the sky near the moon, drooping upon

the sea!

O troubled reflection in the sea!

O throat! O throbbing heart!

And I singing uselessly, uselessly all the night.

O past! O happy life! O songs of joy!

In the air, in the woods, over fields,

Loved! loved! loved! loved! loved!

But my mate no more, no more with me!

We two together no more.

The aria sinking,

All else continuing, the stars shining,

The winds blowing, the notes of the bird continuous

echoing,

With angry moans the fierce old mother incessantly

moaning,

On the sands of Paumanok's shore gray and rustling,

The yellow half-moon enlarged, sagging down, drooping,

the face of the sea almost touching,

The boy ecstatic, with his bare feet the waves, with

his hair the atmosphere dallying,

The love in the heart long pent, now loose, now at last

tumultuously bursting,

The aria's meaning, the ears, the soul, swiftly depositing,

The strange tears down the cheeks coursing,

The colloquy there, the trio, each uttering,

The undertone, the savage old mother incessantly crying,

To the boy's soul's questions sullenly timing, some

(continued)

drown'd secret hissing,

To the outsetting bard.

Demon or bird! (said the boy's soul,)

Is it indeed toward your mate you sing? or is it

     really to me?

For I, that was a child, my tongue's use sleeping, now I

     have heard you,

Now in a moment I know what I am for, I awake,

And already a thousand singers, a thousand songs,

     clearer, louder and more sorrowful than yours,

A thousand warbling echoes have started to life within

     me, never to die.

O you singer solitary, singing by yourself,

     projecting me,

O solitary me listening, never more shall I cease

     perpetuating you,

Never more shall I escape, never more the

     reverberations,

Never more the cries of unsatisfied love be absent

     from me,

Never again leave me to be the peaceful child I was

     before what there in the night,

By the sea under the yellow and sagging moon,

The messenger there arous'd, the fire, the sweet hell

     within,

The unknown want, the destiny of me.

O give me the clew! (it lurks in the night here

     somewhere,)

O if I am to have so much, let me have more!

A word then, (for I will conquer it,)

The word final, superior to all,

Subtle, sent up—what is it?—I listen;

Are you whispering it, and have been all the time,

      you sea-waves?

Is that it from your liquid rims and wet sands?

Whereto answering, the sea,

Delaying not, hurrying not,

Whisper'd me through the night, and very plainly

      before daybreak,

Lisp'd to me the low and delicious word death,

And again death, death, death, death,

Hissing melodious, neither like the bird nor like

      my arous'd child's heart,

But edging near as privately for me rustling at my feet,

Creeping thence steadily up to my ears and laving me

      softly all over,

Death, death, death, death, death.

Which I do not forget,

But fuse the song of my dusky demon and brother,

That he sang to me in the moonlight on

      Paumanok's gray beach,

With the thousand responsive songs at random,

My own songs awaked from that hour,

And with them the key, the word up from the waves,

The word of the sweetest song and all songs,

That strong and delicious word which, creeping to

      my feet,

(Or like some old crone rocking the cradle, swathed

      in sweet garments, bending aside,)

The sea whisper'd me.

From "Sea-Drift"
Leaves of Grass

ACKNOWLEDGMENTS

Edited by S. L. Berry and Nancy Loewen
Photo research by Ann Schwab
Design assistant: Mindy Belter

PHOTO CREDITS

The Bettmann Archive
Culver Pictures, Inc.
The Granger Collection
North Wind Picture Archives
Stock Montage
Winter scene in Brooklyn, New York 1817–20
by Francis Guy. Oil paintings on canvas 4' x 8'1" Museum of The City of New York #53.2

SELECTED WORKS BY WALT WHITMAN

Since the first edition appeared in 1855,
Leaves of Grass has never been out of print.
Whitman revised and expanded the book until
his death; the contents listed below are for the
final edition of 1892.

Leaves of Grass
  Subdivisions:
    Inscriptions
    Children of Adam
    Calamus
    Birds of Passage
    Sea-Drift
    By the Roadside

    Drum-Taps
    Memories of President Lincoln
    Autumn Rivulets
    Whispers of Heavenly Death
    From Noon to Starry Night
    Songs of Parting
    First Annex: Sands at Seventy
    Second Annex: Good-bye My Fancy

PROSE
Democratic Vistas, 1871
Specimen Days, 1882

INDEX

First published in 1994 by Creative Editions
123 South Broad Street, Mankato, Minnesota 56001
Creative Editions is an imprint of The Creative Company.
This title is published as a joint venture between The
Creative Company and American Education Publishing.
Copyright © 1994 The Creative Company.
International copyrights reserved in all countries.
No part of this book may be reproduced in any form without
written permission from the publisher.
Printed in Italy.
Art Direction: Rita Marshall
Designed by: Stephanie Blumenthal
Illustrations by Rob Day
Library of Congress Cataloging-in-Publication Data
Loewen, Nancy, 1964 -
     Walt Whitman / written by Nancy Loewen.
     Includes bibliographical references and index.
     ISBN 1-56846-096-1
     1. Whitman, Walt, 1819–1892—Biography.   2. Poets,
American—19th century—Biography.   I. Whitman, Walt,
1819–1892.   II. Title.
(Mankato, Minn.)
PS3232.L63   1993
811'.3—dc20   93-15081
[B]   CIP